BECOME A PRIVATE TUTOR

HOW TO START AND BUILD A PROFITABLE AND SUCCESSFUL TUTORING BUSINESS

VICTORIA OLUBI

Subscribe to my newsletter for free tutoring tips.

www.thetutoress.com/free-resources

Table of Contents

How To Accidentally Stumble Into a Billion Dollar Industry	*4*
The Nitty Gritty of The Tutoring Industry	17
Bad Tutors vs. Good Tutors vs. Great Tutors	20
The Five Marks of a Great Tutor	23
Choosing Your Subject(s)	28
Marketing Your Tutoring Business	32
How To Handle The Competition	40
How To Create An Income That Works For You	50
Additional Resources for Online Lessons	57
Handling Hagglers	60
Putting it Together	66
The Tutor Plan	68
Final Note	74

How To Accidentally Stumble Into a Billion Dollar Industry

When most people tell you about how they started their businesses, there's usually a description of a light bulb moment, merging of minds or a magical idea. For me, none of those things were the case.

I started tutoring by accident. Yes, by accident.

I graduated from a traditional university where students were expected to build successful careers in 'the city.' Initially, the lure of six figure salaries, long days and high-rise buildings appealed to me but upon graduating, I realized that I was far too creative to be a banker, lawyer, hedge fund manager or stock broker.

I wanted to do something different, something that made an impact on the world in some shape or form whether that be on a local, national or even international scale- I didn't mind.

The problem was that whilst I knew what I didn't want to do, I had no idea what I wanted to do.

After graduation, came that dreaded, 'I need to get a job!' phase - a phase that I intensely detested. Six months later, I had accumulated a pile of rejection letters and was so fed up that I almost gave up entirely. Luckily enough, I managed to get a job at a local school working with special needs children. To say these children were deprived would be an understatement; many of the children were from broken homes and had faced their fair share of difficulties. However, whilst working with the children I quickly discovered that despite all of their problems, they like most children, just wanted to be cared for, respected and treasured.

During my time at this particular school, I was given the opportunity to educate, inspire and empower dozens of children.

Whilst my time at the school wasn't perfect, it taught me a few things about myself and I realised that I was deeply passionate about teaching. I loved coming up with new ideas for lessons, creating new learning techniques to use with the children and I loved the rush that teaching gave me.

There was nothing more amazing to me than seeing a child light up when they finally understood something that had previously baffled them.

There was something about teaching that gave me confidence and eased my nerves.

I loved it and whilst I wasn't completely sure that I wanted to be a teacher, I knew that I wanted a career that involved educating others in some way.

However there was a problem and that problem was the fact that whilst I loved teaching, I hated the school environment.

Grumpy teachers, school politics and handling my new role as an adoptive mother to dozens of children was not my idea of 'fun.' The great teachers were fantastic but the not-so great ones were…difficult.

The reality that I loved teaching but hated the teaching profession hit me when a senior teacher complimented, "you're too good for this school, you should teach somewhere else!"

My teaching skills weren't just noticed by teachers. Parents also picked up on it and asked me to tutor their children but because that was against school policy I politely declined but mentioned that I could teach children from other schools and would really appreciate a referral.

That referral came from a nice young mum who asked me to teach her son English at High School level. He was a witty young boy who was keen to learn but hadn't been given the best foundation in English.

After he passed his exams, referrals came and I soon began to realize that there was an opportunity to potentially make just as much money tutoring as I had done in my teaching assistant job.

Three years after I took on my first ever tutoring student, I'm here today with a thriving tutoring business that allows me to earn a living by making a positive impact in the lives of children and young people from across the world.

I've been fortunate to build a successful tutoring business very quickly and am in awe of the potential that exists for people to earn a living in this industry. However, it hasn't been a simple and smooth ride. I made a lot of mistakes and learnt a lot about the business along the way.

This book serves the purpose of sharing the lessons I've learnt so that you don't make the mistakes that I did and hopefully the advice and tips that I share will help you to acquire the knowledge needed to build a successful tutoring business from the ground up.

> **"The man who can make hard things easy is the educator."**
> **Ralph Waldo Emerson**

Tutor? What's In A Name?

The definition of the word 'tutor' is often misunderstood. When I tell people I'm a tutor, they almost always ask whether I have a qualified teaching certificate or degree. I usually give them a polite response and explain my qualifications and experience very briefly. However, I'm still baffled at the confusion between tutoring and teaching.

A tutor is defined as "a private teacher, typically someone who teachers a single student or a very small group." In comparison a teacher is defined as "a person who teaches in a school." Yes, the definitions might seem similar but they're actually quite different. A tutor is someone who specializes in teaching people (whether that be children or adults) in small group or individual capacities. A teacher however, in most cases has a teaching qualification (usually beyond a degree) and teaches in a school. Teachers are required to not just be experts in their field but to also be excellent classroom managers. Tutors on the other hand are hired for their expertise in a subject as well as their ability to teach in an individualised manner.

Within the state school system, teachers are expected to have specific teaching qualifications (like the PGCE). In private schools however, there is no standard requirement that teachers have teaching qualifications. Essentially, you could be a teacher at a top private school without even needing to have a teaching qualification; in most private schools an undergraduate degree from a good university would be enough.

Most people assume that you need to have a teaching qualification to tutor but in most cases you don't. The majority of tutors are self-employed and are completely separate from the traditional school system.

Furthermore, the tutoring industry isn't regulated which means that almost anyone can be a tutor. If you have a skill in a specific area and don't have a criminal record then you are free to tutor if you like.

The point I'm trying to make here is that so many people could be tutors but feel as if they're not qualified enough. If you want to tutor, there's pretty much nothing stopping you so you shouldn't feel as if you're inadequate. In fact, if you're great at tutoring but aren't tutoring, then you're probably doing the world a disservice by not sharing your knowledge and skills with the world!

Almost anyone can tutor. That includes mums, dads, graduates, teaching assistants, former teachers, former corporate executives and dinner ladies. Tutoring can be a wonderful career choice especially for people who already have experience of working with young people and children. Nonetheless, if you're not a fan of teaching children and prefer to teach adults, tutoring can still be an excellent career choice for you.

One of the things that makes tutoring great is that it's suitable for people who are looking to teach on a full, part or flexible basis. Whether you're looking to earn some extra money for a few hours of work or you're hoping to earn a five-six-figure salary a year, tutoring is ideal for you.

Another great thing about tutoring is that the rate of pay per hour is generally much higher than in other professions. For example, most jobs pay on average £10-£15 per hour. In contrast, tutors can easily charge £20- £100 per hour. In some American cities like New York, tutors charge upwards of £300 per hour! No, that's not a typo. Some sought-after tutors can even earn thousands per day. The demand for tutoring is huge and it's still a relatively untapped market with growing potential.

In this book, I'll share some brilliant strategies for starting and growing a tutoring business that is profitable, enjoyable and effective.

The Nitty Gritty of The Tutoring Industry

I won't bore you with statistics and fact files but I will share a few statistics that matter when it comes to understanding the tutoring industry and the potential that lies within it.

Recent statistics show that the tutoring business is worth an estimated $5 billion dollars globally. Yes, $5 billion! That figure tells us two key things:

1. Tutoring is an in-demand market. In other words, people are willing to pay based on a need. Education is a highly valued commodity and people are willing to fork out big bucks in the hope of achieving academic success.
2. The second thing that it tells us is that there's money to be made in this field. If people across the world are spending $5

billion dollars on something that means that it's a potentially hugely profitable market.

In the UK specifically, the tutoring industry is worth at least £100 million pounds. It's one of the fastest and most consistently growing industries in the world and is amongst a handful of business sectors that are growing every single year.

Let me put that into perspective for you. We're in a global recession and as a result only a tiny proportion of business sectors will see profits. An even smaller fraction will see growth. The industries that see growth are those that are in serious demand. They provide goods or services that people need and can't live without. For example, food, health, transport and…education.

Ok, so those are the good facts that tell us that this is a profitable market. However, I must emphasise one key thing.

To succeed in any industry or any business, you can't just copy what everyone else is doing and expect to compete with established businesses.

To succeed, you must stand out from the crowd and be distinctive. That means that as a tutor you can't create a website or tutoring profile that looks like everyone else's, you have to figure out what makes you unique and leverage that so that parents are drawn to you.

We'll discuss more about succeeding even when there's competition later on but just bare in mind that you must make sure that your branding reflects what makes you different.

> "Always walk through life as if you have something new to learn and you will." Vernon Howard

Bad Tutors vs. Good Tutors vs. Great Tutors

What skills do you need to be a private tutor?

There are two vital skills that you need to be a private tutor. In my opinion, these two skills matter more than any other in terms of making you a great tutor.

The first skill is the willingness to learn. Are you someone who loves to learn new things or someone who gives up when they don't immediately succeed? To be a tutor, you don't necessarily need to know everything that there is to know about a subject. Rather, you need to be willing to learn everything there is to know about a subject. Sometimes you won't know the answer to something but you need to be willing to find it out so that you can learn it and then teach it. In other words, you need to be a student of life, someone who considers themselves a student first and a tutor second.

That willingness to learn, that hunger in your belly is what will differentiate you from other tutors. Be hungry to learn more and be a more knowledgeable person. As a very wise person once said, **"Learners are earners."**

The second skill is the ability to teach. By teaching I don't just mean standing up in front of a crowd and rambling on and on about a subject. That's not teaching! Teaching is the ability to take a complex subject and make it digestible. Can you break down complicated topics? Can you make something that many people might find boring, seem interesting? Can you explain difficult topics using stories, graphics or art?

If you answered yes to any of the above questions then you may well have the potential to be a great tutor.

> "Education is the most powerful weapon which you can use to change the world." Nelson Mandela

The 5 Marks of a Great Tutor

If you want your tutoring business to succeed, you need to strive to be a great tutor. Good tutors attract average clients. Great tutors attract the best clients. Good tutors settle for average salaries. Great tutors earn the highest incomes. Good tutors take on clients who don't value them. Great tutors attract clients who adore them. Which would you rather be?

So what makes a great tutor and how do you become one?

Great tutors possess the qualities I'll outline below. If you're aiming to built a successful tutoring business where you attract fantastic clients then I highly suggest you follow the following:

Punctuality. Being on time makes the world of difference and shows that you respect other people's time. If you're booked to teach a lesson but you're running late, simply call or text the parent to let them know. Don't leave them in the lurch wondering where on earth you are!

The ability to listen. People love people who listen to them. Why? When you take the time to listen to someone else, it shows that you're selfless and self-effacing. If on the other hand, you don't listen to your clients, they'll immediately think that you're self-absorbed and narcissistic. Take time to listen to what they want and find out what their goals are in relation to tuition lessons.

Communication. When a parent contacts you to arrange lessons, don't ignore their call or email for weeks! Communicate with them from the very beginning. That could be by sending a reply to say you're fully booked but would like to put them on your wait list or it could be calling them to thank them for enquiring about your tuition services. Always communicate before, during and after a parent has booked you.

Approachability. I can't count the number of times when a parent has said things like, 'I love the fact that the kids relate to you and see you as being more than a teacher.' Being relatable is a great skill for a tutor to have. Approachability means possessing the ability to relate to your clients and their children. For example, if a student is struggling with understanding a complex Maths equation, take time to understand why they might be struggling to understand this particular question. Try in whatever way you can to relate to your clients and see things through their eyes. They'll value you it forever.

Organisation. Whilst I don't pride myself on being the most organised person on the planet, I am big on being organised and managing responsibility. As a tutor you'll be expected to plan lessons, liaise with schools and teachers, speak to new prospects on the phone, manage referrals and be someone that parents can turn to when they have questions or concerns about their child. It's therefore essential that you get organised. For instance, keep a diary of all your goals for the day, have a calendar on hand and keep track of your daily and weekly duties. In doing so, you'll optimise your chances of succeeding as a private tutor.

Choosing your subject(s)

When people ask me about becoming a tutor, one of the first questions they ask is how do you know which subject to teach?

I believe that you should pick a subject you enjoy learning about and have an interest in. Are you mad about Maths or incredibly passionate about Italian? The more passionate you are about a subject, the better chance you'll have of teaching it well and positioning yourself as the go-to tutor for that particular subject.

Another matter to consider when picking your subject is whether there is demand for it. For instance, if you decide to teach an obscure subject that is hardly taught in schools you might find that very few people show interest in having lessons. However, that doesn't mean that there it's impossible to make money by teaching a unique or unpopular subject, it simply means that you'll need to do your research and decipher whether teaching that subject alone will be worthwhile.

As a general rule of thumb, traditional subjects that are taught at Primary (Elementary) and Secondary (High School) levels are usually the most in-demand. For instance, Maths, English and Science. Maths (at all levels and ages) is probably the most popular subject for private tuition.

There are however, exceptions to the rule.

Take for instance, elocution, it's not taught in schools but it's one of the most in-demand subjects in the tutoring industry. A lot of people want to master their speech and learn how to speak like the queen. Demand far outweighs supply in the elocution market.

Another thing to take into consideration when picking your subject is whether you're genuinely good at teaching it. Teaching is a skill and it requires practice and mastery. Furthermore, some people are brilliant at certain subjects but they're awful at teaching it.

To ascertain whether you'll make a good tutor, it's a great idea to gain tutoring experience before you decide to fully embark on a tutoring career. For instance, you could volunteer to read to children at the local school or you could teach at your local church. Gaining experience is invaluable and will help you to figure out whether a tutoring career is right for you.

> "Doing business without advertising is like winking at a girl in the dark. You know what you are doing but nobody else does." Steuart Henderson Britt

Marketing Your Tutoring Business

Marketing. It's a dreaded word for most people. The thought of marketing a business of any kind can seem like a daunting prospect. However, in the tutoring industry, there are some great ways to market your services. Many of these methods are free or very inexpensive.

Word of mouth

If you're at that point where you've thought about tutoring but don't have any contacts, connections or experience, word of mouth seems like a completely useless approach. Hold that thought! Word of mouth isn't just powerful for people with establishing tutoring businesses, it's also pertinent for aspiring tutors who've yet to start.

To get started, simply let your friends, family members and acquaintances know that you're offering tutoring services and ask them to spread the word for you.

You could even offer them a reward for each successful referral they give you. For instance, if your friend refers two friends and one of them books lessons with you, your friend therefore gets a free shopping voucher.

Offering incentives and rewards is great for creating buzz and getting people interested in your new venture.

If you're an established tutor, you can offer incentives and rewards to existing and previous clients by notifying them of a special scheme you're creating to bring in new clients. Using the idea above, offer them a voucher in exchange for referrals. You'll be surprised at the number of customers who know lots of potential clients and will gladly recommend you.

Furthermore, there are probably people that you already know who are looking for a tutor but have no idea where to find one. By telling them that you're offering tutoring services you'll be encouraging them to take action and get the help that they need. Don't be afraid to tell those around you that you're embarking on a tutoring career.

Another great technique for attracting new clients is to get in touch with local press. Getting featured in the local press is a great way to attract customers. Being featured positions you as a trustworthy local hero who people can trust and turn to.

The press loves a good story so it's important to sit down and think about story angles. For instance, did you recently win a business competition or did you do something remarkable for the local community?

One great way of getting local press is to create an event that makes a difference to local people and invite the press to the event. For instance, you could create a free reading day where you and a group of other local tutors read to a group of children for free. Invite the press along to take photos and interview you. These types of tactics have helped many tutors to establish themselves as local education experts.

Tutoring Websites

In terms of marketing my tutoring business, something that has really worked well for me is to advertise or create profiles on tutoring websites. For instance, the American website NextGuru.com is a great place to advertise on. You can create a free basic advert or upgrade and pay for a low cost ad. It's an excellent way to get enquiries. Whilst it's geared towards American tutors, tutors from other countries can advertise their services. NextGuru.com isn't the only tutoring site on the market, there are plenty of others.

It's worth setting up free profiles or ads on these websites and testing the level of enquiries you receive. If you receive a few good enquiries then that's a good sign that it's worth paying for a full advert. Use your discretion to decide whether it's worth advertising on a particular site.

As a rule of thumb, advertising on tutoring websites shouldn't be expensive, most of the best sites I've ever used have cost no more than £60 per year and sometimes the level of enquiries I've received has been so high that I've had to create a waiting list. Furthermore, if you receive just one client from a tutoring website you'll have recouped the amount that you spent advertising with them. As I mentioned previously, this is a tried and tested method that has gotten me excellent results.

Workshops

Whilst some schools are resistant to promoting private tutors, many will promote you if you offer a free workshop to students and/or parents. Some tutors make most if not all of their income from hosting workshops on topics such as creative writing, geography and chemistry.

Workshops usually involve a tutor giving a presentation on a topic and then giving the students fun activities to do. Teachers love workshops and many schools are happy to have tutors or education providers host workshops for a few hours during periods such as the summer and winter terms.

To promote your tutoring service you could offer the workshops to schools for free in exchange for them handing out your brochure or leaflet. Conversely, you could charge for your workshops. The average cost of a workshop in the UK is £300, which is about $460. Not bad for a day's work.

By the way if you're interested in learning about more marketing methods for tutoring subscribe to my free newsletter at **www.thetutoress.com/free-resources**.

Charging Fees and Handling Competition

It's so easy (and common) to see people start a business and base their prices, branding and services on what their competition is doing. This is a completely false approach. If you want to have a successful tutoring business then it's essential to do two things:

1. Watch, research and observe what your competitors are doing.

2. Then, ignore them!

I'm sure you're thinking, 'what on earth does she mean?' or 'how can I ignore my competitors when they're competing with me?' keep reading.

Before you start your tutoring business, it's worth doing a bit of research and checking up on who your competition is and how much they charge. You can do this by simply Googleing words like 'private tutor London' and see who comes up. What sort of tutor are they? Are they a company, franchise or individual? How much do they charge?

Using the information provided on their websites write down the answers to the above questions so that you have the information you need on hand.

Now, the next thing to do is to research one key thing. This 'thing' is essential because it allows you to figure out how you'll position your tutoring business.

The key 'thing' or question to now ask is: who is the target market of your competition? Who are they marketing to? Is it big corporations, wealthy middle-eastern executives or wealthy businessmen?

Now compare their target market to their pricing. Are they targeting less wealthy people and charging low fees or wealthy people and charging high fees?

Once you've found out the information you need, keep it on one side.

The reason why I advice ignoring your competition is because when you visit tutoring websites like The Tutor Pages or NextGuru.com, you'll come across a lot of tutors who charge very low fees. Whenever I used to see the prices that other tutors charge, I'd feel upset or anxious because they were basically charging pennies for what seemed like the same service I was providing.

I knew that to survive I couldn't charge as low as they did. I needed to differentiate myself by charging a fee that reflected my value. This is key! Your price reflects your value and how you see yourself. If you honestly think you're a worthless tutor who's inexperienced and unknowledgeable then charge £5 per hour. But by the time you travel to the student's house, teach and travel back, you'll have spent far more than £5 teaching the lesson. Why teach just to lose money? It just doesn't make sense.

Of course there will always be tutors who charge £5 per hour. They charge low prices because they're afraid of not getting enquiries and they're worried that people won't pay more for their services.

Sometimes, some of the low-charging tutors are genuinely inexperienced and charge low because their goal isn't to make a proper income. They simply want to built up experience and get testimonials to use for future clients. This is actually a great strategy for new or aspiring tutors who have no experience and want to build up their contacts, connections and referrals. However, for established tutors, you shouldn't be charging low fees because it undermines and undervalues your skills and achievements as a tutor.

That brings me to a little story about my own experiences. A few years ago, I was asked by a wealthy, upper-class family to teach their daughter. I spoke to the mum on the phone and said that my fee was £30 per hour. She said, 'that's far too cheap!' I was completely in shock because most parents in my area refused to pay £30 for an hour's lesson. To cut a long story short, a few months after teaching the lady's daughter, I met up with another London tutor and she mentioned that she knows a tutor who charges £100 per hour. I couldn't believe it. That seemed like an extremely high amount of money for a lesson. However, it turned out that the tutor charging £100 per hour was working for the same family as me. No wonder why she thought I was cheap! I could have tripled my fee and it wouldn't have bothered her in the slightest.

See why pricing makes a big difference?

Now in terms of ignoring the competition, here's what I mean.

In business we often follow what our competitors do to the extent that we mimic everything they do. We assume that by making our branding look similar to other brands, we'll look more professional. Quite the opposite is true.

Your clients (whether they be schools, companies or individuals) are bombarded with choices in terms of who to hire. Every tutor looks the same to them and it's difficult for them to who's or great if everyone has branded themselves in the same way.

To make yourself stand out you need to be unafraid of branding yourself differently. **How do you do that?**

Ensure that you do all of the following:

✓ Have a website that stands out from the crowd. It should look professional whilst showing off your business's originality.

✓ Embed your personality into your website and your marketing materials. A great way to do this is to use photos (of yourself or your students) on your marketing materials.

✓ Communicate clearly what you do. What's your unique selling point as a tutor/ education provider? State clearly what makes you different or better than other tutors.

✓ Get your website visitors to subscribe to your mailing list or newsletter in exchange for something free. For example on my website **http://www.thetutoress.com**

✓ I state why parents and tutors should join my mailing list.

✓ Have an 'About' page that states what you do and how you help people. For example, "I'm Miss Olubi and I am a private tutor from London. I help students to pass 11+ and private school entrance exams. I also teach English classes where I help people to improve their speaking skills and communicate more effectively." Your 'About' page should clearly communicate what you do and how you help people.

✓ Have testimonials or letters of recommendations, which act as proof of your services.

How To Create An Income That Works For You

As I mentioned previously, pricing is a sensitive and complicated subject in the world of business. Often when we're pricing our services we feel uncertain, unsure and make brash decisions based on what our competitors are pricing.

We know that pricing similarly to our competitors isn't the best approach but how do we therefore figure out how to price our tutoring services?

There are different approaches and schools of thought. Here are some to consider or follow:

Option 1: The work backwards strategy

Let's say that you want to earn £30,000 per annum for your tutoring services.

Let's imagine that at the moment you're charging £30 per hour for your one-to-one tutorials. That means that in order to earn £30k you would need to teach for 1,000 hours during the course of a year.

That's an awful lot of tutoring.

You might then decide that rather than charging £30 per hour, you could instead increase your prices to £40. That would reduce your teaching time to 750 hours and leave you with 250 hours of time to travel, relax or spend time with family.

Option 2: The Group Option

Group classes are a brilliant idea especially because you can charge for instance, £10 per hour per child and have up to about 10 children in the class. The smaller your class sizes, the more you can charge parents per hour. So a class of just 5 children would allow you to charge something like £15 per child rather than 10. Always do the Maths and see which pricing strategy is best for you.

Option 3: Going virtual

I used to do most of my teaching in-person or in small groups. However, the problem with face-to-face lessons is that they require travelling from place to another and take up a lot of time.

Furthermore, teaching face-to-face meant that I didn't earn any income whenever I was too ill to work.

The advantage of teaching online is that there are no travel expenses, it's unbelievably convenient and both the student and teacher can work in an environment that is comfortable and familiar.

When I first started tutoring, I assumed that there wasn't much demand for online tuition but nowadays more and more parents are becoming aware of the benefits of having an online tutor. In many ways it's a win-win situation.

Option 4: Online Classes

There's definitely potential for you to transition into online classes or have online tutorials that compliment the lessons you already provide.

For example, if schools/ parents have contacted you requesting tuition lessons but you're fully booked, it's pretty much a waste of money telling those people that you're fully booked and can't take them on. Instead you could create an online programme where you simply record your voice and teach using a screencast or PowerPoint presentation.

How do you do that? It's really not that difficult. You simply need a free tools and resources:

A microphone that's either in-built into your computer or one that you can purchase from stores like pc world. Simply tell the staff in any computer store that you're looking for a microphone or headset that works with computers and they'll happily help you to find one. Most computers have in-built microphones but sometimes the quality is better on an external microphone.

2. Create course content that covers the topics you'd teach in one of your lessons. For instance, 'phonics for kids' or 'pronunciation for kids.' Then start planning content that fits in with the title.

3. Create a PowerPoint presentation and record your voice using your computer. Using PowerPoint it's easy to add your voice to the PowerPoint presentation and then you've created a video tutorial.

4. Upload your teaching materials online. You can create a private YouTube channel where only your students can see the videos you've created (and not the public). Once they've paid for your content you can send them a YouTube link to your video. Once you upload your video to YouTube there's a button to press where you can make your video private and then

send the links to your students via email. It's very straightforward.

Additional resources for online lessons

These are my tried and tested favourite resources!

Camstudio.org. This site allows you to record your computer screen live so that students can see your computer and you can also record your voice.

Screencast.com. You can get an account for free and record the screen on your computer. It makes teaching online very easy!

* Wiziq.com. This is my absolute favourite resource for teaching online courses. There are over **1 million students on the website** and they're hungry for teaching materials and have the money to spend on them! There are only about **200,000 teachers** on the site, which means that your chance of finding students is high. You can also try it for free for 30 days so there's no expense involved. This is an excellent site for tutoring online because many of the students are international/foreign and are eager to learn English. Some will even pay for classes where they just speak to an English person! All you have to do is create 'hot topics' conversations like 'Where do you live?' 'Do you like movies?' etc.

TutorsNirvana.com.   Although   it's relatively new, Tutors Nirvana looks like a promising option for tutors who want to teach online. It's also one of the most affordable providers of online tuition software and the staff are friendly and helpful.

* Curatr.co.uk is another great site for creating online courses and an online virtual classroom.

I've put a **(*)** next to the sites that I personally think are the best for tutors.

> "The key to charging more is knowing how to properly convey your value." Ramit Sethi

Handling Hagglers

As a tutor, I often receive enquiries whereby parents, teachers and schools are reluctant to pay a certain fee for my classes or lessons. Some will do anything to save money or avoid paying the full cost that I charge.

I used to just accept that this was part of the job and that some people wouldn't pay the fees I was charging. However, as I've become more experienced I've realized something.

People claim that something is too expensive for them but they also spend a lot of money on things that aren't important. For example, the mum who says she can't afford tuition lessons for her son but spends £100 getting her nails done. Or the school that says they can't afford your workshop but spend thousands on materials that don't help their students to get better results.

The reality is that people often say they can't afford something when in actuality they can!

The fact is, if you really want something, you'll find the money to pay for it even if it's a bit pricey or out of your budget.

So, how do you overcome the "you're too expensive or I can't afford you" excuse?

It's simple.

Express and communicate clearly the value that your classes or tutorials can bring.

For instance, if a parent says that lessons with me are too expensive I respond: "my lessons might seem pricey but they reflect my expertise, experience and value. The fact is that I get students into top schools, I am one of the only tutors in London who coaches children for interview practice and I include all of my materials in the cost of my lessons. You therefore save money by hiring me because if your child gets a scholarship for a leading private school, you won't have to pay £20,000 a year on school fees. By hiring me you're saving thousands."

Usually, after saying that, parents are begging to book lessons with me.

As you can see in the example above, communicating value is about focusing on the long-term benefits that your services provide. For instance, if a parent said that your lessons were expensive you could respond with something like, "my lessons are excellent for because they help children to improve their confidence and help to enhance their passion for learning." The more you practice communicating value, the better at it you become.

When you express value, people realise that you're worth every penny and more. I can't count how many parents said initially that I was too expensive and now call me to say that my lessons are a bargain. They now realise how valuable private tuition is.

Lesson: Don't accept the "I can't afford you" excuse.

Some things to include when talking about benefits are:

- Long-term savings. For instance, will lessons with you help your client to save money in the long run?

- Opportunities. Will your tuition lessons increase people's job prospects? Will it increase their income or chances of getting into a top school, a good job or a prestigious university?

- Your expertise. Are you the leading tutor in your area? Do you have glowing testimonials from clients who love your work? Can you name any high-end/prestigious clients?

- Your value. What benefits do your classes bring to the client? How can it help them? As Seth Godin states, 'people always want to know what's in it for them.' Tell the client what benefits they'll receive.

Putting it together.

Now that we've covered the benefits of tutoring, how to pick your subject, and options for tutoring, it's time to put everything you've learnt together.

I've created a plan on the next page that will help you to map out your ideas and will aid you in strategizing your plans for building a hugely successful tutoring business.

When you complete The Tutor Plan, base your 'dream client' on the person who will pay for your tutoring services and not the student themselves. For instance, if you teach ten year olds, your dream client won't be a ten year old but the parent of one.

Try to be as detailed as you can when filling in your Tutor Plan. Once complete, take some time to create a visual image of what your tutoring business will look like. You can do this by creating a vision board on Pinterest.com or by simply getting a large sheet of paper and sticking on images that represent your dream tutoring business.

The Tutor Plan

Name:

_____

Date:

_____

1. I want to be a tutor because I want to:

2. The age group I'd like to teach is:

3. The subject I'd like to teach is:

4. My main skills are that I am:

5. I'd like to teach online/in-person/through workshops or a mix of the above. List the ways in which you'll teach:

6. My main competitors are: (include their names and website addresses)

7. I'm different from my competitors because I provide: (what services or offerings do you provide that your competitors don't?)

8. My absolute dream client would be: (Think BIG and be as specific as possible. For instance, would you work with diplomatic families, teach Maths to a star athlete or be the go-to tutor to wealthy families in Dubai?)

9. My dream client reads the following 5 publications: (include websites, newspapers and blogs)

10. My dream client hangs out or spends their time at these places: (include networking groups, events and clubs or societies that your dream client is a member of)

11. To connect with my dream client I will do these 5 things:

12. I'm willing to connect with other tutors and business owners in order to spread the word about my services. The 5 businesses/tutors that I'll connect with are:

13. To bring in a constant stream of referrals I will do these 5 things:

14: If I could have the most amazing tutoring business possible it would be located in _____ and I would specialize in teaching _____. My business would be unique because it would cater to

_____.

Congratulations!

You're now on your way to growing a successful tutoring business that's fun, profitable and that makes a difference in the lives of others.

Whenever you're feeling uncertain, go back and read through and answer the questions above.

Final Note

Remember, growing a successful tutoring business takes time. It took me at least a year to go from one client to several and then another year to go from having a decent number of clients to being so booked up that I needed a waiting list.

Ongoing Support

If you'd like more detailed support on growing your tutoring business, make sure you subscribe to my tutoring newsletter at **www.thetutoress.com/free-resources**.

As a member of my newsletter you'll receive free updates and exclusive access to coaching and support that will help you to build a truly remarkable tutoring business.

I wish you the best of luck with building your business and I hope to keep in touch with you through my newsletter. You're also welcome to send me a tweet @TheTutoress.

Yours sincerely,

Victoria.

Author, Become A Private Tutor.
Founder of TheTutoress.com
www.twitter.com/thetutoress

Notes

Use this space to write down any notes or ideas that you have.